You Don't Live on My Street

Rebera Elliott Foston M.D., MPH

Copyright © 1991 Rebera Elliott Foston M.D., MPH
All rights reserved. No part of this book may be reproduced without written permission.
Library of Congress Catalog Card Number: 91-91930
Edited by: Cynthia Elliott Garnett Ed. D., Roscoe Fleming
Cover Illustration by: Will Foston M.D.
Text Illustrations by Rebera Elliott Foston M.D., MPH

Forward

I wish to thank Almighty God for allowing me to be the vessel through which He allowed these words to pass.

I want to dedicate this book:
to my late father,
Mr. Frank M. Elliott, who taught me how to dream
to my mother,
Mrs. Erma Elliott, who taught me how to love
to my sisters,
Verneva, Eleanor, Cynthia, & Portia, who cleared the path to excellence for me,
to my brother, Thomas, who pushed me to achieve,
to my husband, Will, who always believed in me
to my sons, Bryan and Amia, who never allowed me to get discouraged,
to my nieces and nephews, whose laughter nourished me,
to my friends, who never allowed me to doubt myself,
to the teenagers of the Foston Adolescent Workshop, Inc. who provided a stimulating and creative environment for me,
to my staff at the Gary Health Department, whose enjoyment of my work encouraged me ...
but most of all
to the thousands of teenagers, who have touched my life, and whose cries have been lost to the night.

Table of Contents

I. POOR

Love Filled In the Gaps	10
My Neighbor	11
A Real Good Time	12
No Love	13

II. HARD

Black Woman	16
Little Orphan Boy	17
At the Top of the Stairs	19
It Ain't Gettin' Any Better	20

III. RESPONSIBILITY

The Business of Being Black	24
I Don't Got the Time	27
Mister Social Activist Man	28
The Business of Being a Woman	29
You	32

IV. ALONE

You Are Not Welcome	36
I Don't Know How	38
You Know How It Is	39
I Am Sorry	41
If I Could	42

V. STAYING ALIVE

Leaving Too Soon	46
DisIntegration	50
It Wasn't That Bad	51
Living In Fear	53
You Don't Live On My Street	57

VI. SELFLESS

Gotta Get My Smiling Eyes Back	64
Mama, I'm Sorry	65
Slow Down Chile	66
So I Thought	67

VII. SPIRITUALITY

A Family	70
Look for the Butterfly	72
All We Have Is Now	74

VIII. DIFFICULT

The Armour	78
It Is A Shame	80
Do You Feel It?	81
Afraid	82
Ain't No Use	83

IX. SELF-LOVE

The Awakening	86
My Emotions	87
So When Is It Love?	88
Come Inside	90
I Feel Fine	91

X. DETERMINATION

Standing In the Gap	94
One Monkey, My Show	95

Introduction

Rebera Elliott Foston M.D. MPH has always loved to write poetry. She managed to include some creative writing courses in her studies at Fisk University, but her passion for writing soon became overshadowed by her technical studies. She graduated Magna Cum Laude, Phi Beta Kappa, in Biology from Fisk. Then she received her medical degree from Meharry Medical College in Nashville, and her Masters Degree in Public Health from the University of North Carolina, in Chapel Hill. She became a Board Certified Family Practitioner, with an emphasis in Adolescent Health Care, and received her Post Doctoral Fellowship training in Family Medicine, at Michigan State University, in East Lansing. She is presently the Health Commissioner for the City of Gary, Indiana, where she was born and reared.

Her passion for writing poetry, however, reemerged shortly after she dedicated her practice of medicine to "Adolescents Only" in 1985. In that same year she created the Foston Adolescent Workshop where she has helped over 1200 teenagers to feel good about themselves by giving them the time, space, and latitude to hone their musical, writing, acting, speaking, critical thinking, and caring skills. However, it was after she had heard and treated the real pain of over 15,000 teenage patients, and their parents, that she decided to try to capture some of this pain on paper. Already hundreds of teenagers have heard and been visibly touched by her poetry.

Dr. Foston's current goal is to create a home that can house hundreds of teenagers who find themselves not being parented. This home will be called "Somewhere" (There's A Place for Us). A portion of the proceeds from this book as well as from all of the Foston Adolescent Workshop projects will be directed toward making this goal a reality.

Dr. Rebera Elliott Foston would like for you to read and hopefully enjoy this manuscript. She hopes that some poem or passage may touch you, help you, heal you, amuse you, strengthen you or move you in some way.

Will Foston M.D.

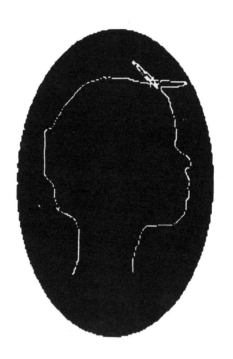

Individual as each
flake of snow
as Black women our lives
intertwine so
In a faded dress
waiting on the sun
in this Black woman's book
POOR is CHAPTER ONE

Love Filled in the Gaps

Sometimes we didn't
have much money
When we ran out of sugar
we just used honey
And sometimes the grits
were a little runny
But Love filled in the gaps

There didn't always seem
to be enough time
the meat we ate
wasn't always prime
And sometimes we didn't
have but a dime
But love filled in the gaps

Sometimes we had
holes in our socks
Couldn't always afford
to curl our locks
And had the beans
without the ham hocks
But love filled in the gaps

We always seemed to
make our parents mad
And peace of mind
they never had
But we were happy
more than sad
Because love filled in the gaps

My Neighbor

May I borrow
A cup of your strength
A dollar of your time
and a few inches of your shoulder
on which to cry

May I borrow
A cool drink of your kindness
As I freshen up my ideas
And kick off my shoes of depression
for a while

May I borrow
A loaf of your advice
Even though I can only
handle it a slice at a time
for now

May I share
some of my burden with you
Just let me rest here a minute
And I'll be all right

Thank You

The world gets so heavy sometimes

A Real Good Time

Mary, ain't you supposed
   to be in school today
I'm twelve, but I can't
   read anyway
How you spendin' yo' days
   Now don't be lyin'
I'm just looking for
   A REAL GOOD TIME
Seems like yo' life
   done hit the skids
You just fifteen now
   and got three kids
I'll try to help
   if you in a bind
Watch my kids so I can
   find me A GOOD TIME
Yeah, welfare took
   my kids for now
Leaving kids alone
   they don't allow
I just went to the store
   to get some wine
I didn't know I was
   gonna find me A GOOD TIME
Mary, chile
   is that you?
It's been five years what
   you been up to?
Don't come at me
   with that tired old line
Ten dollars can get you
   a REAL GOOD TIME

No Love

Love must have left
Long fo' Mama died
You know somethin'
I still haven't cried
My Dad used to beat
Mama so bad
Beating was the only love
Mama ever had

When she passed away
It was my turn
I had to do things
I hadn't even learned
I had to cook,
wash and clean
and he treated
all of us mean

The oldest of ten
I just happened to be
so all the responsibility
fell on me
I left with the first man
that I found
and he turned out to be
a drunken clown

I had five kids
before I could breathe
So the first chance I got
I had to leave
I ain't no kinda of Mama
there ain't no doubt
I'm just twenty-five
but I'm plum wo' out

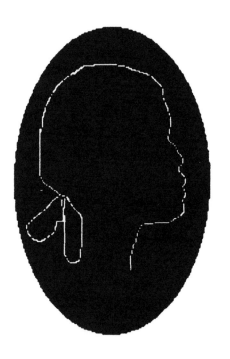

A Need that will
not sit still
A Want ready to
explode or kill
A growing anger
that is not new
In this Black woman's book
HARD is CHAPTER TWO

Black Woman

Black Woman!
I know that I'm meddlin'
But why are you settlin'?
On yo' head he's beatin'
And on you he's steady cheatin'
Black Woman!
Black Woman!
To your man you go crawlin'
then there you go bawlin'
And I just want to know
How low will you go?
Black Woman!
Black Woman!
Why you out here raisin hell
while one son is in jail?
You know the other son is sellin'
So why ain't someone you tellin'?
Black Woman!
Black Woman!
I know that I'm dippin'
But child support he's skippin'
You know you out here workin'
While he's somewhere off jerkin'
Black Woman!
Black Woman!
How can you be willin'
to leave all yo' chillin'?
And what can you be thinkin'
when you doin' all that drinkin'?
Black Woman!
Black Woman!
You know things just ain't right
So you must stand up and fight
and you must understand
you are the only one who can
Black Woman!
Come On
Black Woman!

Little Orphan Boy

Little Orphan boy
How'd you get this way
with your Mama and Daddy
living somewhere today
You see my Mama
is goin' wit' cocaine
and now she don't even
know her name

My Daddy's he's done
married alcohol
and now he ain't fit
for nothin' at all
My Mama's mama
she's a sweet ol' girl
I wouldn't do nothin'
to hurt her in this world

But she ain't been the same
since big Daddy died
She won't talk to me
Lord knows I've tried
My Daddy's mama
she stays low sick
since they cut off her foot
and she walk wit' dat stick

My Daddy's Daddy he
stays on the go
chasin' wine and women
well you know
My Mama's sisters
they are very mean
like they don't like
a living thing

18

They say what's happened to Mama
serves her right
When big Daddy messed wit' them
She didn't fight
I got plenty of uncles
and one got a wife
they got they hands full
wit' they own life

I don't like staying with them
cause if the truth be known
None of them know how
to act like they grown
They cuss each other
and beat they child
So I just had to get
away for a while

I told my caseworker
it wasn't my fault
That I was picked up
by the police for assault
You see I'm thirteen,
the gun was a toy
And I'm just a
little black orphan boy

At the Top of the Stairs

At the top of the stairs
There are toys everywhere
expensive dolls and stuffed bears
in a sweater
At the top of the stairs
are fine dresses to wear
things to touch ? No one dares
You know better!

At the top of the stairs
No one combs their hair
as they decide what to wear
on their own
At the top of the stairs
breakfast no one prepares
The rod no one spares
is all they've known

At the top of the stairs
the sound of thrown chairs
is heard amidst the swears
and the fighting
At the top of the stairs
huddled in despair
are tear soaked eyes, two pair
in dim lighting

At the top of the stairs
Joy and laughter are rare
As if no one cares
it's a bad dream
At the top of the stairs
As if they are unaware
What can't survive up there
is self esteem

It Ain't Gettin' Any Better

It ain't gettin' any better
We just gettin' older
Yo' boyfriend's still actin'
bolder and bolder
You let him whup yo' head
then cry on my shoulder
It ain't gettin' any better
We just gettin' older

It don't make no sense
He ain't treatin' you right
You payin' the rent
He spendin' the night
Everyday you getting ready
either to cuss or to fight
It don't make no sense
Yo' eye swole with no sight

It's just plain crazy
year after year
You havin' his babies
Me cryin' each tear
You livin' in pain
and nothin' but fear
It's just plain crazy
things ain't what they appear

It just ain't right
He's actin' prouder and prouder
He's drinkin' again
gettin' louder and louder
You tryin' to cover those scars
with more and more powder
It just ain't right
please ya'll don't crowd her

I just can't stand it
could you please be for real?
How can you go on
lovin' him still?
If you don't kill him
One day I will
I just can't stand it
Is it just a cheap thrill?

I hope you leave him this time
for treatin' you this way
Puttin' up with his lyin'
day after day
Him callin' you names
No matter what people say
I hope you leave him this time
Each night I pray

It's truly a shame
Everyone but you can see
Us livin' this life
I wish he'd let me be
'Cause when he ain't hittin' on you
He's feelin' on me
It's truly a shame
We should be free

It ain't gettin' any better
He's actin' colder and colder
He's shootin' up again
This time the cops had to hold her
You see that's my Mama
Lord knows I done told her
It ain't gettin' any better
We just gettin' older

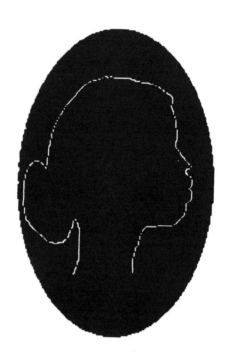

Too much, too soon
too often again
No disgust no fighting
no arguing will win
In this Black woman's book
CHAPTER THREE
is all about
RESPONSIBILITY

The Business of Being Black

When you gonna start buying what
you need instead of always stealing
And get off all that liquor
and all that dope dealing
And stop sellin' the little
children all that crack
cause that's the business of
being Black

When you gonna stop sellin'
your body for the right price
Life holds so much in store
You can still claim your slice
Try a job that keeps
your self respect intact
cause that's the business of
being Black

When you gonna marry that woman you
been living with all these years
Who's had each of your babies
And calmed all of your fears
try bringin' home some groceries
regularly in that sack
cause that's the business of
being Black

When you gonna stop clowning
And put that man out
Making your children wonder
what death's all about
If he wants to belittle you
tell him to pack
cause that the business of
being Black

When you gonna stop looking down
on your brother with a curl
While you feelin' on the butt
of the new office girl
And try building some ego
you surely lack
cause that's the business of
being black

When you gonna stop politickin'
and doing all that grinnin'
makin' all those hollow promises
and doin' all that skinnin'
Get people decent housing
instead of a shack
cause that's the business of
being Black

When you gonna stop worrying
about who's got more than you
See what's real in life
And who you can help too
And stop demanding
he up more and more jack
cause that's the business of
being Black

When you gonna stop gossiping
cause you sad and lonely
causing constant confusion
and thinking of you only
Try not always being
so out of whack
cause that's the business of
being Black

When you gonna stop complaining
And go on and teach
A decent future for our kids
is way out of reach
And try givin' each Black child
a little more slack
cause that's the business of
being Black

When you gonna wake up
and see the importance of school
Instead of skippin', cheatin'
and actin' a zip dummy fool
Try learning instead of polishing
your verbal attack
cause that's the business of
being Black

When you gonna stop profiling
and preach God's word
Make sure children are seeing
Just what they heard
And keep everyone spiritually
on the right track
cause that's the business of
being Black

When we gonna live up to
God's master plan
Putting our life entirely
In His hand
And stop stabbing each other
in the back
cause that's the business of
being Black

I Don't Got the Time

Hey Baby, You sho' look fine
Naw Baby, that ain't no line
Here Baby, try some of this wine
Yeah Baby, you sho' is prime

Find a job? You know I been tryin'
A baby? Chile you must be lyin'
Where have I been all this time?
Wait now are you sho' it's mine?

In to the kitchen, start some fryin'
Another woman? There you go pryin'
Wish you'd stop yakkin' and whinin'
Be back soon, No I ain't lyin'

The hospital? Look like you dyin'
Not now! Me and the boys be flyin'
Naw Chile, I don't got the time
Excuse me ! Can you loan me a dime?

Mister Social Activist Man

Hey, Mister
Social Activist Man
Carryin' that big sign
in your hand

"Free Africa?"
Is that you plan
Your ideas
are oh so grand

You volunteer in
soup kitchens each day
And tell each person
it will be okay

You cheer them up
when they are down
And cry when someone
sleeps on the ground

But Mister Activist Man
you know it's been a while
When was the last time
you've seen our child?

While you marching
up and down the street
Remember your baby
needs something to eat

So Mister
Social Activist Man
Tell me something
I don't understand
How will you feel
If the battle is won
And you can't remember
the name of our son?

The Business of Being A Woman

The business of being a woman
is to be Daddy's little girl
in a safe and protected world
waiting for a Duke or an Earl
Is the business of being a woman

The business of being a woman
is to forever be her daughter
She was crying and you caught her
seeking comfort and you sought her
Is the business of being a woman

The business of being a woman
is to be a good natured sister
Knowing you will always miss her
the very best you always wish her
Is the business of being a woman

The business of being a woman
is to feel that you are needed
to give advise even tho' not heeded
To wear that dress, white and beaded
Is the business of being a woman

The business of being a woman
is to be by your man's side
never to run and never to hide
from the turbulence of the tide
Is the business of being a woman

The business of being a woman
is to be someone's mother
and to protect them like no other
and to carry your heavy brother
Is the business of being a woman

The business of being a woman
is to know what to do
And somehow always on the right cue
And without even so much as a clue
Is the business of being a woman

The business of being a woman
is to do what is right
No matter how cold or hot the night
til the trouble is way out of sight
Is the business of being a woman

The business of being a woman
is to be your man's best friend
and to be loving until it's the end
Sympathies to him you then extend
Is the business of being a woman

The business of being a woman
is to learn to cry alone
and to make it on your very own
and without being very well known
Is the business of being a woman

The business of being a woman
is to sing your own song
Working, slaving all the day long
Teaching children right from wrong
Is the business of being a woman

The business of being a woman
is to inspire trust
and live life fair and just
and to believe in yourself you must
Is the business of being a woman

The business of being a woman
is touching the petal of a flower
and from injustice never to cower
Understand and use your full power
Is the business of being a woman

The business of being a woman
is to choose to ignore
those who'd destroy your very core
and to embrace the ones you adore
Is the business of being a woman

The business of being a woman
is to remove all limitations
and to tolerate no imitations
and to understand the situation
Is the business of being a woman

The business of being a woman
is to learn all you can
and basic respect you must demand
On important issues, take a stand
Is the business of being a woman

The business of being a woman
is to fight for your dream
No matter how hopeless it may seem
Have a place where you can scream
Is the business of being a woman

The business of being a woman
is to lead the way
No matter what other people may say
and to always kneel down and pray
Is the business of being a woman

You

You were my feet
Until I could dance
to my own music

You were my legs
Until I could stand
alone

You were my hands
Until I could feel
my way

You were my arms
Until I could hold
myself up

You were my shoulders
Until I could carry
my own burdens

You were my heart
Until I could love
myself

You were my skin
Until I could cover
my vulnerability

You were my voice
Until I could tell
my own story

You were my eyes
Until I could see
justice clearly

You were my ears
Until I could hear
the symphony

You were my beliefs
Until I had my own
disappointments

You were my ideas
Until I could think
for myself

You were my confidence
Until I could believe
in myself

You were my reason
Until I could decipher
truth

You were my mirror
Until I could see
my own reflection

You were me
Until you set
me free

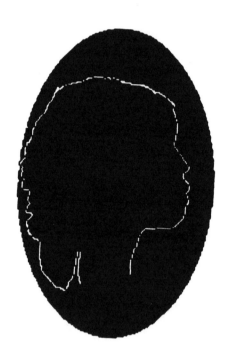

Wounded still with
children to protect
Seated amidst the
notices of disconnect
Tears passing each other
as they race to the floor
In this Black woman's book
ALONE is CHAPTER FOUR

You Are Not Welcome

You are not welcome
And Baby that's for real
The same way your family
has made me feel
They would say things
to hurt my pride
And you would always
take their side

I'd be cookin' tryin'
to make somethin' taste good
Yo Mama'd say "Chile
this ain't as good as I could"
When I'd go shopping
then ya'll would start
Sayin' can't she find somethin'
to fit at K-Mart?

I'd ask for a mink
You'd say git a rabbit
Is being cheap hereditary
Or just a force of habit
Where do you get off
thinkin' you know
What's good enough for me?
Man, that is low

Then yo' sisters would
lay in the cut
sayin' how did Sonny
wind up with that slut
Your brothers would be laughing
You'd be in it too
Slappin' hands saying I wasn't
as fine as Mary or Sue

If the chicks you dated
were all that fine
How come none of them
fell for your tired line
They were all smarter
than me in one thing
None of them was dumb enough
to get stuck wearin' yo' ring

I've decided it's over
and it's about time
'Cause I've been abused
by your family and mine
I was thinkin' being with you
was doin' me some favor
But yesterday I stared
all day at your razor

I knew somethin' else
had to be done
When I found myself staring
at your loaded gun
We both need help
So we can try again somehow
But we've got to rearrange
this derangement right now

I'm more than willin'
to meet you half way
But we have to start
tryin' harder today
But if you want to leave
please, don't be amazed
That your broke-down door
swings both ways

I Don't Know How

I'm sitting here lonely
without a man
My children are all grown
each with their own plan
As a single parent I've
struggled up until now
I need to be an adult
but I don't know how

Of all the pieces I've given
of my heart
I don't know where
I left the last part
I've always given everyone
so much of me
I'm disappearing
Can't you see

I used to have aspirations
dreams and desire
But I've had to keep my balance
on the high wire
Like a butterfly
I need to shed my cocoon
But what if the winter
has come too soon

I feel like a child
taking her first step now
And if I fall,
I'll get up somehow
Whatever it is
I feel I can do it
I'll be glad when I
no longer have to prove it

You Know How It Is

I just wanted him
to feel like a king
a symbol of our love?
I didn't need a ring
to tell the truth
I thought of no such thing
But you know how it is
when you try to love somebody

I just wanted him
to know how much I cared
demand commitment
I never dared
these new feelings
had me very scared
But you know how it is
when you want to love somebody

I just wanted him
to fill all my needs
I asked no papers
to be decreed
I just wanted
our love to succeed
But you know how it is
when you have to love somebody

I just wanted him
to believe in my worth
Trapping him?
My last thought on earth
I cried out his name
as I was giving birth
But you know how it is
when you need to love somebody

40

I just wanted him
to be by my side
I asked no knots
to be tied
just to look at his
child with pride
But you know how it is
when you should love somebody

I just wanted him
to check on us now and then
to see his baby's first steps
or his similar grin
or the beautiful dimples
in my baby's chin
But you know how it is
when you got to love somebody

I just wanted him
to know it has been a while
the support papers
I had to file
I'll need a little help
raising my child
But you know how it is
when you can't love somebody

I just wanted him
to know there has been no strife
because I never
got to be his wife
My child and I
have had a wonderful life
But you know how it is
when you don't love somebody

I Am Sorry

I am sorry
I cannot be
Everything you
Want me to be

I tried walking
behind you
But my strides
were too long

I tried waiting
for you
But Time told me
that was wrong

I tried heeding
you
But that put me
where I didn't belong

I tried needing
you
But I found out
you were not that strong

I tried singing
back up for you
But the World
had to hear my song

I'm sorry
I cannot be
Everything you want me to be
But I just have to be free

If I Could

If I could love you
   for about a year
   I would convince you
   to please stay right here
   beside me

If I could love you
   for a month or so
   I would try to get you
   not to go
   away from me

If I could love you
   for about a week
   I would try to reach
   my sensual peak
   just for you

If I could love you
   for only a day
   I would show you
   that there's no way
   you could leave

If I could love you
   for even an hour
   I would try to use
   all my will power
   to keep you

If I could love you
   for just a minute
   I'd put all
   my emotions in it
   so you'd stay

If I could love you
   for a hot second
   I would try to
   get you just to beckon
   me to you

If I could love you
   for a moment long
   I would try to forget
   that it was wrong
   and hold you

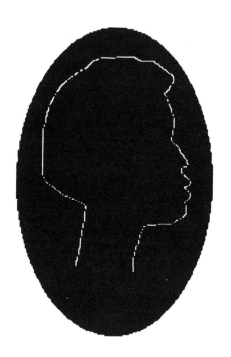

Trying to hold on
while taking life's curves
just getting rebalanced
and again having to swerve
In this Black woman's book
CHAPTER FIVE
is all about
JUST STAYING ALIVE

Leaving Too Soon

Can you tell me why
a little black baby
Reaches his first birthday
only maybe
Alcohol, poor nutrition
or cocaine
somehow become
his middle name

Too little prenatal care
Is being sought
Too little health education
Is being taught
Can we stop this dying
months from the womb
Cause too many Black babies are
leaving too soon

Can you tell me why
this little Black child
hasn't been bathed
or fed in a while
As a society
aren't we supposed to protect
these children from dying
of abuse and neglect?

Too little parenting
is being learned
Too little education
is being earned
When can we stop
this sadness and gloom
cause too many Black children are
leaving too soon

Can you tell me why
this young Black teen
is lying here dead
at this accident scene
Her friends say
she didn't have any pride
and was always
talking about suicide

Too much information
Black teens need to know
Too few helping places
where they can really go
She was supposed to
graduate in June
But too many black teenagers are
leaving too soon

Can you tell me just
what is the answer
to keep Black women
from dying of breast cancer
Is there any way
to get the message across
before any more lives are
senselessly lost?

Too few appointments
for mammograms
too few doctor visits
for all health exams
Sitting beside her
in the hospital room
Too many Black women are
leaving too soon

Can you tell me why
it's the Black man's lot
to stand a good chance
of being shot
Something else to try
to understand
Why the killer will probably be
a Black man

Too few fathers, jobs
and good intentions
Too many women, drugs
and legal detentions
When can we stop
singing the same sad tune
and keep our Black men from
leaving too soon

Can you tell me why our elderly
find staying alive
difficult past the age
of sixty-five
with this gap in death rates
we should be displeased
Especially when the death
is from a preventable disease

Too much time with grandkids
is being lost
the quality of life
is at too high a cost
This situation should
make us fume
cause too many Black elderly are
leaving too soon

Can you tell me just
when will the Black race
put health first
in its rightful place
Instead of keeping up
with the family called Jones
making sure our health status
is regularly known

Too much time is spent
trying to impress
Too little time to take
a simple blood test
Can we hurry and change
this prediction of doom
and stop Black people from
leaving too soon

DisIntegration

When you choose
to assimilate
You then spontaneously amputate
yourself from the richness of the
mighty, moving river of
Blackness
that is the mother of all that is
Humanity

When you choose
to ignore who you are
You become nothing and none of the
Beauty, Determination, Hope and
Love from that mighty river can
pass
through you to your children who
then whither

When you choose
to turn your back on all that is
real, you become like an
undeveloped negative amid the rich
colors of the Fall's palette and
you become afraid of the
sound of your own
laughter

It Wasn't That Bad

I'm sixty-nine, and you can't judge
the kind of life, I've had
Well, I'm telling you here and now
It really wasn't that bad
When we first called ourself dating
At each party, he was the show
And all the women there
Oh, how they envied me so

Not until after we married
A little heavier he would drink
And maybe once in a while
he'd throw up in the sink
Back then he'd only hit me
If I had done something wrong
Like the time I forgot
to leave the night light on

Once I left him three whole months
and took our little baby
but without me he said
he almost went crazy
After I had four more babies
he really started to change
He started staying out all night
and coming home acting strange

He may have hit all the children
sometimes a little too hard
But he didn't mean to burn me
with that skillet of hot lard
We had to run out for our lives
Only once or maybe twice
But everyone in the church
thought he was really nice

He never missed a day of work
and that house note he paid
and for the next fifteen years
we really had it made
Daily drinking, or his temper
I don't know which came first
But when that mean boss fired him
Everything just got worse

For five years I tried everything
the more things would fall apart
He would pass out everyday
and it would break my heart
All my children even started
telling stories on him
Telling me that each night
he was messing with one of them

Now, none of my three daughters can
handle any of their men
and both of my two sons
are somewhere drinking again
They always keep on blaming him
and me for all of their pain
Why one doctor tried to tell me
one of my sons is insane

Well, I'm tired of this family
putting all this off on me
I don't want to rear their children
I wish they'd let me be
My husband, he's dead and gone now
So I'll speak for their Dad
Our life with him, I'm telling you
really wasn't that bad

Living In Fear

I don't think I can
make you understand
what it has been like
living with this man
Some things I could tell you
you would be shocked
Some things are so painful
they have my memory blocked

If I had known he was like this
when we first met
I would have stayed as far away
from him as I could get
I hate him, I love him
it feels so queer
But I just can't stand this
living in fear

You never know
what he'll do or say
Let him get some help
each night I pray
I know I married him
for better or worse
But I can't stand
the way that he'll curse

No one cares if he
threatens me with a gun
Each day I live my life
Wondering where can I run
Watching him kill himself
drinking year after year
But I can't stand always
living in fear

I wish I could
make you understand
What it has been like
living with this man
I guess cause I'm the oldest
So mean he would treat me
When he got through hitting Mama
then he would beat me

Whenever he's awake
he will scream and yell
And sometimes I think
that there is no one I can tell
Each day I feel
that I've cried my last tear
Cause I can't stand having
to live in fear

He gets mad even
if I talk on the phone
and sometimes I think
that I am all alone
Mama tells me all the problems
his drinking has caused
and sometimes I wish
there were stricter laws

She keeps telling me
that one day we'll all leave
But I've heard it so often
no more can I believe
I've thought of killing myself
and I am sincere
Cause I just can't stand having
to live in fear

If only I could
make you understand
What it has been like
living with this man
You never know if he's
gonna come home drinking
You wonder if you want him home
You sit there thinking

You see I'm his only son
and my life is so grim
Cause I wonder if I'll turn out
like grandpa and him
To tell you the truth
I can't stand being here
Cause I hate to have to always
live in fear

You don't know how it feels
to have your dad the town drunk
Especially when you realize
how low his life has sunk
Each time he hurts my mama
a part of me just dies
He says he's gonna straighten up
Huh, another one of those lies

I think about all the bad times
Each time I smoke a joint
Like the time he held our whole
family at gun point
J&B and I are friends now
although I started with beer
Cause I just can't stand always
living in fear

You will never
be able to understand
What it has been like
living with this man
Cause I'm the youngest
no one pays me any attention
and the things my daddy's done
to me I'm afraid to mention

I guess cause my Mama and I
look a lot alike
He'll be coming into
my bedroom again tonight
I'm the most afraid
when he's drunk and trying to steer
and I really can't stand always
living in fear.

You just cannot feel anymore
your soul is numb
you can't do well in school
and everyone calls you dumb
I don't know if it is worse
when Dad is home or away
Mama stays so upset she won't even
let me go out to play

He drinks, but I've got to
get us all help somehow
I think I'll start
by calling AA right now
I feel like my mother
and father I have to rear
and I can no longer stand
living in fear

You Don't Live On My Street

So you want to know
Why I'm always high
and why you never
ever see me cry?
Why do I shoot up
all this junk?
Have you ever seen
Your Dad sloppy drunk?

Sure I would like
to have more knowledge
but my Dad drank up
my money for college
So, how can you look at me
with such conceit
When you don't even live
on my street

So you want to know
why I ran away?
Why in boarded up buildings
I'm hiding each day?
You want to know why
I choose to steal
and do what I have to
just to get a meal?

Well I don't worry any more
about getting good grades
all I worry about now
is getting AIDS
Look at you with your
life so sweet
but you don't live
on my street

You ask me why at fourteen
I'm having this baby?
Am I ignorant, retarded or
just plain lazy?
What on earth
was I thinking about?
I was hoping my Mama
wouldn't put me out

See your Mama's boyfriend
ain't messing with you
and putting his hands
on your little sister too
Naw, the seventh grade
I didn't complete
But, hey, you don't live
on my street

So you want to know
Why I dropped out of school?
How many times can you
be called a fool?
Ever since first grade
I been called slow
So I wouldn't give the answer
even if I did know

An how was I supposed
to concentrate
When I can't remember
the last time I ate
Do you live everyday
with defeat?
Then you don't even live
on my street

You ask me why I
stay with him
when he beats my head
again and again?
You want to know why
I don't get upset
when he makes each
drunken idle threat?

Well do you have rats
running cross your head
when you lay down
in your broke-down bed?
Do you have shoes to
cover your feet?
Then you don't live
on my street

You want to know why
I'm not raising my chile?
Well, you know
I ain't worked in a while
You want to know
why I don't keep in touch?
Is buying some Pampers
asking too much?

Can I start coming
'round the place
I'm ashamed to let
my chile see my face
You s'posed to get out of the
kitchen if you can't take the heat
So, naw you don't live
on my street

You don't know
a thing about me
but there are some things
that you must see
Until you have walked
in my shoes for a while
and had a taste
of my lifestyle

Until you have lived
in my house
and given a name
to each mouse
Until you've seen
your Mama get beat
You don't even live
on my street

Until you have walked
my walk
Until you have talked
my talk

Until you have knelt down
on my knees
Until you have eaten
my government cheese

Until you have smelled life through
my nose
Until you have worn
my panty hose

Until you have seen life through
my eyes
Until you have worn
my dress size

Until you have heard life through
my ears
Until you have cried some of
my tears

Until you have lived inside
my head
Until you have laid down in
my bed

Until you have read what's on
my mind
Until you have stood in
my welfare line

Until you have been called out of
my name
Until you have felt some of
my shame

Until you have sold some of
my dope
Until you have lost all of
my hope

Until you have stood under
my rain
Until you have felt some of
my pain

Until you have eaten
what I've had to eat
then understand this
You don't live on my street!

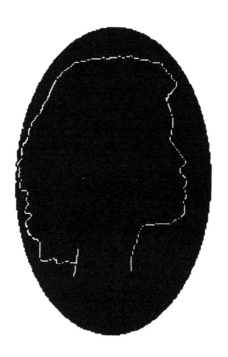

With demands forcing the back
into an awkward arch
everyone else has their tune
for us to march
others broken dreams
we are trying to fix
In this Black woman's book
SELFLESS is CHAPTER SIX

Gotta Get My Smiling Eyes Back

People say I'm witty
and laugh real hearty
Yes everyone thinks
I'm the life of the party
Ever since I was
a little bitty child
I've tried to face the
world with a smile

But you could look
into my eyes
And see my smile
was full of lies
You took one look
not even two
But the hurt in my eyes
could not fool you

I don't know how
you could see
I'm so alone
It even scares me
What are you
supposed to do
when you're not sure
if anyone loves you

My face is smiling
you say my eyes are not
But this mask of pretense
is all I've got
I've got to get my life
back on the right track
I gotta get
my smiling eyes back

Mama, I'm Sorry

I'm sorry if I
sometimes make you mad
But Mama, there are reasons
I act so bad

If I say I want something
you'll say it's just a fad
If I do something good
you are never glad

Each time I get a girlfriend
you get mad
You act like I'm the only friend
you've ever had

I know you are always lonely
and so very sad
But you've got to
ease up just a tad

I'm only fourteen
just a little lad
Your age when you got knocked up
by that cad

Eventhough I'm the first
child you ever had
I'm sorry Mama
But I'm not Dad

Slow Down Chile

Slow down, chile
You movin' too fast and if you ain't careful
You might even pass
Me

Hold back chile
Cause if I let you attain
How am I ever gonna explain
My Lie

So excuse me
While I cut you down
And try my best
to shut you down
Now

Give up chile
Cause if I let you achieve then
Who will ever again believe in
Me

So I Thought

The glow of a candle
burns brightly, dims,
and then fades...
Or so I thought

But the glow of our love
grew brighter and more
intense each day...
Or so I thought

Then you left

Winds were not supposed to blow
Nor was the sun supposed to shine
Or so I thought

But when I
admitted,
believed,
understood,
accepted
We could not be

Winds blew again
the sun shone and
the day slid into the night's path

and my pulse beat again

Or so I thought

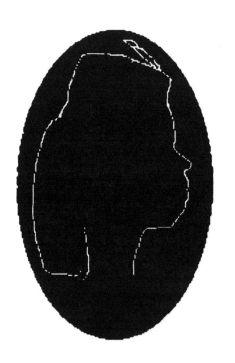

Guided by a belief
in things not seen
and having only God
on whom we can lean
Needing to know
there is a Heaven
In this Black woman's book
SPIRITUALITY is CHAPTER SEVEN

A Family

In the back room
kids were playing Nintendo
and old men noting
how much the kids did grow

In front of the TV
were some in their teens
And another group talking
of different college scenes

So many names,
I'll never remember
Each with enough likeness
to still be a member

Nurturing and caring
four generations strong
Fellowshipping and storytelling
all night long

The middle age folks
were all still round the table
The men convincing them
that they were still able

To laugh the loudest
or recall the farthest back
With plenty of jiving
with no harm or attack

Both young and old women
expressed similar hope
And shared imaginative ways
of trying to cope

Eating food until everyone
felt on the brink
With everyone dodging
their turn at the sink

Each one genuinely
enjoying each other
Every sister
and every brother

Remembering all
of the times gone by
And little boys sneaking
another piece of pie

Everyone jumps to give
Big Mama a ride
when her sore feet
get the best of her pride

Eventhough big Daddy
died this past spring
Their circle of caring
forms a continuous ring

And the power of their love
shone round and about
and of one precious thing
there is really no doubt

For future generations
one, two and three,
This will always
be a beautiful family

Look for the Butterfly

When you're feeling low
and below you is nowhere
When life has dealt you a blow
and you really don't care
Look for the Butterfly

When over, becomes under
and what you've won, you've lost
When happiness seems so far away
and at too high a cost
Look for the Butterfly

When up is suddenly down
and your world starts to break
Good turns into bad and
you've had all that you can take
Look for the Butterfly

Look for the Butterfly
One of God's beautiful creatures
To refocus your world
Study its delicate features
Until there is Hope
Look for the Butterfly

When what seems so right
quickly turns out wrong
You thought you fit in
But didn't belong
Stare at the Butterfly

When someone else
sets limits on you
and you feel there is
nothing you can do
Stare at the Butterfly

When you have lost your
sense of direction
and no one is around to
offer you protection
Stare at the Butterfly

Stare at the Butterfly
Pay close attention to its movement
Keep staring and studying
until you feel some improvement
Until there is Joy
Stare at the Butterfly

When you have to battle
on every front
and the world's coldness
you feel the brunt
Follow the Butterfly

When self doubt
steps in to seek and destroy
When belief in yourself
is just a decoy
Follow the Butterfly

When self pity can sit
across from you and smile
and nothing you do
seems worthwhile
Follow the Butterfly

Follow the Butterfly
on its flitting path
From flower to flower
in the storm's aftermath
Until there is Love
Follow the Butterfly

All We Have Is Now

We cannot change
the past
or the word
spoken last
nor reverse any tear
we've cried
not even if
we tried

We cannot change
a dime we didn't earn
Or choices made
because we didn't learn
Nor any milestones
we did not reach
Or times we didn't listen
to what was preached

We cannot change our lives'
past imprecisions
or our moments of doubt
and indecision
Nor the happiness
we could not find
or yesterday's
frame of mind

We cannot change
what people will say
or the times we
forgot to pray
But we must live life
As full as it will allow
Because all we have is
Now

We cannot predict
what will make us shout
Or know what tomorrow
will be all about
Nor anticipate
who will really care
Or who we can trust
If the weather isn't fair

We cannot predict
if the sky will be blue
Or if the new job
is going to come through
Nor if our friends
will heed our warning
or indeed if we will
see the sun in the morning

We cannot predict
which battles we will lose
Or whose feelings
we will unintentionally bruise
Nor who we will have to
help make it through the night
Or who will be ready to
hold up the light

All we know
is God gave us today
And if we will listen
He will show us the way
So we must live life
as full as it will allow
Because all we have is
Now

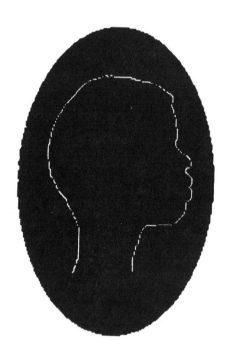

Fighting for the right
to be alright
and finding the way
when the path is void of light
Being prepared
but having to wait
In this Black woman's book
DIFFICULT is CHAPTER EIGHT

The Armour

From the first day
until early retirement
Black man you live
in a hostile environment

You don your heavy armour
all covered with spicules
And try to avoid all
the constant ridicules

You are always the one
who's the permanent object
of problems found
to be wrong with a project

If you have some successes
you sure can bet it
Someone less qualified
will get all the credit

Eventhough we are routinely
paid less than you
Black women have to
put on our heavy armour too

We are expected to deal
as a matter of course
But without any
Single, solitary resource

We hear you as you
begin to rave and rant
When we can get and keep
a job, and you can't

Discussions drag on
about who has it harder
Which turn to attacks
of who's actually smarter

The real problem begins
as we prepare for sleep
One of us forgets
and on the armour we keep

Trying to get closer
is out of the question
This clashing causes
spontaneous combustion

We have somehow developed
this awful mentality
That this armour
is tied to our sexuality

Contrary to what we hear
on the evening news
this disgusting situation
we did not choose

If our love has a chance
to survive anymore
All armour must be checked
at the front door

When we can admit to this game
we're caught up in
maybe then we can meet
again, skin to skin

It Is A Shame

It is a low down, dirty shame
I'm telling you my pain
and you calling it a game

When will we ever try to see
the reasons, and there are three
into this conjugal misery

By my therapist I am told
First of all, I was not whole
when I left my family fold

Secondly, neither were you
Which explains the things you do
You know what I'm saying is true

Thirdly, what we must face
and admit without disgrace
We have taken our children's place

The damage done there's no telling
with all our screaming and yelling
The need to stop is compelling

One more word before I'm through
When I proudly said, "I Do"
It was not a game, I assure you

Our children hurt, we're to blame
So what good is fortune or fame
Let's begin to heal or it's a shame

Do You Feel It?

The sudden burst of laughter
when we talk
The occasional weak-kneed feeling
when we walk

Hoping that the phone
will soon ring
Having the urge to tell you
everything

Wanting to smell your
special scent
Wanting to know what
each sigh meant

Smiling when there's nothing
to smile about
Feeling at any time that
you could shout

Blushing and giggling no
need to pretend
Wishing moments with you
would never end

Being content any place
you take me
Do you see how happy
you always make me?

Wanting to be with
only you
Do you feel it?
What are we gonna do?

Afraid

You let me sit
and fill your ear
with any of my dreams
or words of cheer

It still strikes me
as very queer
that what I want to say
you want to hear

You understand
in ways so dear
all my private thoughts
and things I fear

So I tremble
each time you're near
when I touch you, I think
You'll disappear

Ain't No Use

Ain't no use of you crying
over milk that was spilt
Cause you only operating
out of a sense of guilt
Ain't no use of me trying
all of this to explain
Cause yo' mem'ry is short
I can't make it more plain

If you remember, we
started out fine
with me tryin' to please you
all of the time
Then it seemed like each year
I was pregnant with no shoes
You'd git up and leave
say I was singin' the blues

I'd cook a nice dinner
You'd come home late
with a smile on yo' face
sayin' you already ate
So as soon as I figured out
you was runnin' around
I decided to come home
and just sit on down

Cause if I got to share you
with a woman or two
I'll be damned if I'm gonna
cook and clean for you
I'll admit your actions
took me to school
But I don't have any more
time to be your fool

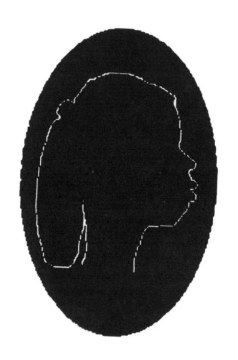

Mirroring the image
of an accurate reflection
and loving it
after introspection
Untying all the ties
that bind
In this Black woman's book
SELF-LOVE is CHAPTER NINE

The Awakening

Having locked them away so neatly
And forgotten them so completely

Tucked them away all snugly
I sat peering very smugly

Then came a sudden rumbling
and an intense grumbling

Hardly recognizable
Barely realizable

All covered with dust
And feelings of mistrust

Protecting their vulnerability
Disguising their humility

Exploring timidly and with caring
the limits of the sharing

They came slowly and sparingly
Then bolder and daringly

Then having their own way
They came out to play

Basking in the warmth of my smile
With wonder like a child

Other feelings they are beckoning
Soon will come a day of reckoning

Having been hidden for so long
returning ever so strong

If I am not mistaken
My feelings have awakened

My Emotions

I am envious of how they
   romp and frolic, carefree
   and rich
   with time
I am jealous of how they
   can hug and touch and
   so completely
   intertwine
I am upset about how they
   can make passionate love
   until
   they drop
I am mad about how they
   can spend all day together
   and no one makes
   them stop
I am hurt about how they
   can know just because
   they choose
   to know
I am livid about how they
   can hold each other
   and never have
   to let go
I am angry about how they
   can so selflessly
   let their
   feelings pour
But I am happy
   they have found each other and
   don't have to be hidden
   anymore

So When Is It Love?

It is love when
   you don't need each other
   and you can laugh easily
   with one another

It is love when
   two people can share
   anything, anytime
   anywhere

It is love when
   respect is a must
   and each one has
   the other's trust

It is love when
   neither one is diminished
   and each one has
   their own work to finish

It is love when
   there's "enoughness" of the heart
   whether you're together
   or apart

It is love when
   sometimes you cannot breathe
   And if it would be better
   one of you would leave

It is love when
   you instinctively know
   what it takes to help
   the other grow

It is love when
    you care about the same things
    waiting for what the next
    conversation brings

It is love when
    you share a particular smile
    and each can carry
    the other's load for a while

It is love when
    there is no surprise
    when you see that look
    in the other person's eyes

It is love when
    you can listen and also hear
    the other person's
    silent tear

It is love when
    you both can see
    the butterfly inside the other
    that needs to be free

Come Inside

Come inside
  my mind to see
  how I feel
Come outside
  and smell the flowers
  that I planted
Come between
  what is and what
  ought to be
Come around
  to see why sometimes
  I cry
Come forth
  to be counted
  as one who cares
Come past
  the doubters who think
  things cannot change
Come up
  to the performance heights
  of the sky
Come down
  to feel
  the green clover
Come through
  the clouds of doubt
  and indecision
Come with
  me as we journey to the limits
  of our capabilities
Come towards
  the bearer of truth
Come away
  with a sense of fulfillment

I Feel Fine

I don't know about you
but I feel okay
Cause I'm not worrying
about nothing today
Especially not about
what I weigh
Aah I feel
Okay

I don't know about you
but I feel nice
Gonna get on with livin'
at any price
Cause I can turn a head
not once but twice
Hey, I feel
Nice

I don't know about you
but I feel good
Cause I'm taking care of
what I should
If I could do better
then I would
Yeah, I feel
Good

I don't know about you
but I feel fine
cause I'm not falling for
your sad line
And I don't owe
nobody a dime
Ooh, I feel
Fine

Yeah, I feel just
Fine

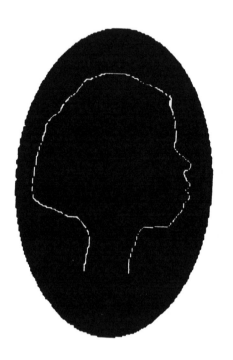

No mole hill, no man,
and no mountain
can stop the creativity
of our flowing fountain
Bring on Impossible,
we are ready to begin,
Cause in this Black woman's book
DETERMINATION is CHAPTER TEN

Standing In the Gap

On my shoulder
came a tap
without a warning
and without a map

It was no joke
It was no trap
Next thing I knew
I was standing in the gap

I felt so bare
without a wrap
sometimes the abuses
felt like a slap

After a victory
there was no clap
I was all alone
standing in the gap

Some blows were hard
and felt like a strap
When I was weary
I couldn't even nap

I'm told I was chosen
because I was apt
And I am still
standing in the gap

One Monkey, My Show

Well, I've got to raise
my children all alone
Cause the man I married
won't stay at home
My Mama keeps telling me
that I'm stupid
and insists on playing cupid

I've made the best
decision I'm sure
and I will find
a way to endure
I refuse to get
discouraged though
Cause one monkey
My show,? No! No! No!

I think I need to
go back to school
But my friends keep
telling me I'm a fool
Because I won't give up
one friend I've lost
But I will succeed
and pay the cost

The more and more
resistance I've met
The more and more
determined I get
So separate ways
my friend and I'll go
Cause one monkey
My show ? OOOOOOOOOOOOh No!

I need to leave this
job very soon
I don't know
if I can stand it 'til noon
Eventhough I am the
best qualified
My boss said he'd
promote me. He lied

Now he's smiling
saying I'll be next
But I know
exactly what to expect
His power over me
I did not bestow
Cause one monkey
My show ? I don't think so!

I need to start
my own business today
But my father keeps
telling me "Ain't No Way"
The reason he says
is so I won't fail
But not trying
is like being in jail

The more I succeed
the more he gets mad
I finally understand
and it's very sad
So onward and upward
I must go
Cause one monkey
My show ? Hell No!